W9-BOB-083

A Doctor's Dose of Inspiration

What a dermatologist learned from
his patients and his life —
wisdom from the skin in.

Volume 2

by Roger T. Moore, MD

Dermwise™

A Doctor's Dose of Inspiration—Volume 2

Copyright © 2020 by Roger T. Moore, MD
Published by Dermwise™
Elkhart, Indiana, United States

Dr. Moore's Main Office Location
at time of publication in 2020 is:
DermacenterMD—Elkhart
111 North Nappanee Street
Elkhart, Indiana 46514
(574) 522-0265

www.DermacenterMD.com

ISBN 10: 0-9600631-1-6
ISBN 13: 978-0-9600631-1-6

Cover image iStockphoto

Contents

Acknowledgements

The patients who walk through the doors of our practice are truly special. Each makes me a better person. Our bond is the magic ingredient and inspiration for this book and so much more. Thank you.

A special note of thanks goes to every health care provider and patient who refers others to our team. We are honored and humbled to receive your trust.

As book editor Tammy Barley helped bring these stories to life. She has been a champion and is a true professional.

Last but not least, my wife Amanda has been the anchor of my life, our practice, and our family. She, like many wives and mothers of today, do **so much more** than what is expected of them. She *is* my **"so much more."**

Introduction

Many years ago a wonderful woman who came into my office told me that every person has a story. She explained that each of us has unique experiences, circumstances, and environmental influences that shape us into who we are.

Over time I have learned what she meant by her comment. We all carry with us moments, struggles, and victories, which all too often remain hidden away inside. Our families, friends, and coworkers never really get to see that part of us.

But something magical takes place when we hear about the struggles and victories of others. It makes people more human and allows us to connect with them on a far deeper level. A bond can be formed, one that can have a lasting impact on our life.

More people than I can count have influenced me through their stories, their actions, and their words. Most of these people will never know that I continue to think of them even years later. The little part of them that has been left with me is something I am humbled and honored to carry forward.

The pages that follow hold just a few of the extraordinary insights from people, books, and life that I have shared in our newsletter over the years. These mini stories remind me that the wonder and power of the human spirit is very much alive and thriving.

I cannot thank each patient enough for being someone who has helped me become just a bit better for the next person who walks through the doors of our office and into my life. It is my sincere hope that as you read the following stories, you will find an invaluable nugget in each that you can carry with you too.

Our journey in life is more than what we take from it. The adventure of everyday living is often the gift we give to others.

We may never know the full results of our efforts. One kind comment, one good deed, or one compassionate moment might be the seedling from which much magnificent fruit grows. So, simply remember that you are unique, truly special, and someone who makes a genuine difference to those in your world.

I wish for you and those you care about all the good that life can bring. At the same time, may you find the opportunity to give and receive the kindness our world should be filled with.

Many happy returns on your good heart, words, and actions.

Enthusiastically,

Roger

Roger Moore, MD

Seed Cans

Hello, My Friend,

If someone has ever told you "you can't," then you are like most of us. In many families and schools, those two words are told to children over and over throughout early life. As one grows older, "you can't" isn't used as much, since most people have learned to follow the path of least resistance.

Yes, the words can be used as a guide to help a child avoid danger. However, the same two words can be demoralizing when they are used to hold back and restrict, or when used at the wrong time.

Only through the experience of life do we find out the hindrances that might have been put on us by others, or the hindrances we are putting on those around us. At times withholding approval or support may be just as damaging as saying or suggesting "you can't."

Henry Ford once said, "Whether you believe you can or you can't, you're right." If each of us lent a hand, gave support, or encouraged one person each day, the seeds planted might very well grow fruit that makes the world around us better than we could imagine.

Commit to telling someone each week "you can" or "I believe in you." That might be just the words they need to begin something life changing for them.

The funny thing is when each of us becomes an "I can" person, others may very well see us differently too.

I know *you can*.

Oddly Inspiring

Someone once asked if any teachers had inspired me. I can honestly say that several made a positive and lasting impact on the development of who I am today. I am so appreciative and fortunate to have had great teachers, coaches, and mentors. The time and effort of every teacher is of immeasurable valuable to society.

My sixth-grade teacher inspired me in an unusual way. Mr. Wahlman asked me to talk with him after class. While all the other kids went out to recess, he sat me down in front of him. My knees shook and my lips quivered as I answered his questions. We had just moved to town the year before, and I wanted badly to fit in with the class. At the same time, I was shy and a bit intimidated by the teacher who I barely knew.

He asked me what I wanted to do outside of class time. I said I wanted to play sports, knowing that was what the popular kids did. I was dying to be liked and believed if I could only play football or basketball really well, the other kids would accept me. As the tension subsided in our conversation, my teacher's tone changed.

We both looked out the window to see our class enjoying recess, playing ball and running freely. He told me, "Roger, very few of those kids will make it to college through sports, and I don't think you will be one of them. Now, if you look at the handwriting here on your paper, it's obvious you need to put more effort into your penmanship and your homework."

His words cut through me, destroying the path I had seen for myself. I wondered if I would ever fit in.

At times I've thought back to that moment as a guide and tool. Though it did hurt to hear his words, they created in me a drive to prove him wrong. Sure enough, I outworked many people in my class, got solid grades, and earned a football scholarship.

My penmanship never did win awards, but thankfully I wound up a doctor where bad handwriting seems to be acceptable.

Sometimes in life people mean well but say things that sting. It's up to us, not them, to decide our fate, our path, and our future. Keep your head up, and keep moving toward your goals.

Don't Miss a Beat

"Every day is a heartbeat. Don't miss a one." That's the message Marshall Sellers repeatedly told his students while teaching high school.

After he revealed the quote to me, he went on to share the passion he had for guiding students to build the best life they could. A foundational block for his message was personal accountability. He believed each child had a great deal of potential, and he was not afraid to tell the children this. He also told them that as a teacher he could only do so much, and that each child had to step up and do his or her part. It's when a person has self-confidence (sometimes aided through the support of others) and personal accountability that one's potential can be fulfilled.

Communicating life lessons was as important to Mr. Sellers as the topic he was required to teach. Discipline, focus, and goals were part of his curriculum. At the same time, he wanted his students to know that each day's work added up to something bigger. Though we might not see the results at the present, the studying, practicing, and effort we make daily creates a sum total of who we become as a person.

In recalling his conversation, I couldn't help but think about how his words can apply to each of us. A famous person once stated, "The best time to plant a tree was twenty years ago. The second-best time is today." Regardless of our age or stage in life, the opportunity to do something meaningful isn't lost. It's only waiting for us to begin.

Start today and build what you will be proud of. "Every day is a heartbeat. Don't miss a one."

Weighing Opportunities

A failed job attempt tipped the scales. That's right. A mistake made fifty-eight years ago by a wonderful man drastically altered the course of his life and those of his future children.

This gentleman in his youth responded to an advertisement for a job. When he walked in to apply, he was told, "This isn't the type-setting company you were looking for. This is the scale company." However, the scale company just happened to be looking for a general laborer. He was told that if he wanted their job, he could come back the next day and start work. And that is what he did. (He didn't even go over to the other company to fill out an application.)

He was the lowest man on the totem pole, beginning his career at the long end of a shovel and using his back to carry heavy items.

Each day he worked to master his assigned tasks. He studied the questions "why, how, where, and who" and gained keen insight to the answers. His diligence began to pay off. He learned so much about the business that his responsibilities grew year after year.

When the owner of the business decided to retire, he could think of no better person to take over his company than the man who had started at the bottom and worked his way up.

Our friend went to the bank, borrowed money, and took up the scales venture. His attitude of quality, service, and hard work provided a way of life for himself and now the next generation, as his boys are following in his footsteps.

His story reveals how the opportunities we are given might very well seem, or frankly *be*, a mistake. It's up to us to make the most of the situations we are presented with. A positive attitude, a willingness to do menial tasks, a knowledge-seeking disposition, and good old-fashioned grit can open doors that others around us might not see.

May your tomorrows be filled with doors that open to new opportunities.

Babe Ruth at the Plate

In an audio I listened to, the speaker noted that what we think about we become. The reference didn't suggest we could become a toad by thinking about it, but rather we can find success if we think about it. At the same time, we can find failure if we focus on it too much.

The world and media today seem to highlight extreme successes, such that it can create a delusional perception for us average folk.

Lost in the world of sensationalism is the fact that many people work hard, falter often, and find their ultimate success in helping others.

After striking out, Babe Ruth was reported to have returned to the dugout with a smile and a chuckle. One of the teammates asked what he thought was so funny about striking out. He replied, "That pitcher doesn't know it, but I'm one at bat closer to my next home run."

Now whether that is true or not I don't know. The story does remind us one of the greatest baseball players in baseball history had way more failures than successes when he batted. At the same time, he is still viewed as one of the greatest hitters of all time.

How many of us would be better off if we could accept ourselves for who we are? Accept our failures or mistakes as events, rather than let them define us almost entirely?

We are designed to be individuals who learn from errors, chuckle at life's challenges, and meet the next difficult spot head-on.

Remember that you are special, able to do great things, and are meant to be the best you that you can be. Keep your head up and make a positive impact on those around you every day. You will find great success in your life.

Hard Road, Awesome View

A psychiatrist, Dr. M. Scott Peck, wrote the best-selling book *The Road Less Traveled*. Though it sounds as though he wrote about a journey he'd been on, like a vacation, he actually shared insightful facts about life.

He started his book discussing how people often blame something or someone for their lack of success, or the perceived bad luck they've had. (I'm as guilty as anyone for thinking at times that the weather, someone else's network, or some other factor was the reason I felt like the world didn't do me justice.) This thinking, though, was one of the first issues Dr. Peck said a person must find truth in before happiness is realized.

He went on to state "LIFE IS HARD," but that there is no easy button, no path without challenges, resistance, or obstacles. Often the perceived golden rainbow of retirement is even met with health, social, and financial obstacles one never dreamed would happen.

Dr. Peck describes how, when a person actually accepts and appreciates the truth of the three words LIFE IS HARD, the person then transcends a level most never achieve. From there individuals can strive toward the best joys life can offer while understanding that pains are part of the path.

Though I have yet to meet a person who truly has an easy life, especially when you see the challenges they deal with each day, I have met some who seem to make life appear peaceful. Those people are the ones who are most likely taking the lumps given and making the best of them.

As you and I pass through our days, I wish you the strength to handle your challenges and also plenty of restful moments to appreciate the joys.

Enlightened

If you have worked with a mentor, then you've received guidance to ease your path. Mentors help propel and ease another person's journey to make life easier than if they had to go it alone.

At times mentors aren't people you know firsthand, but rather people you learn from through books, audios, or videos. In this way some mentors have continued to provide insights even after they've passed away.

One man, Jim Rohn, has been a mentor to many people through his teachings. In one of his audios, he explained the term *philosophies*. What are philosophies? They are the beliefs and thoughts that not only guide who you are but also how you react to situations that come your way.

It's easy for most of us to get sour and blame other people, situations, or entities (like the government) for our current state of affairs. Mr. Rohn taught that in this wonderful world, "For things to change, we must first change." He explained how our mental outlook (attitude), approach, and belief system are largely what determine our outcomes.

If we're willing to work first on ourselves and see things in the most positive light, the negative outcomes we anticipate may very well be changed. It is our inherent belief system, or philosophies, that drive results, good or not so good.

If you find a situation leaving you a bit disenchanted with another person or in a challenging circumstance, try examining why you feel negatively. If you determine that your outlook might be causing some of the tension, see what changes you can make in yourself. The changes you make within will often lead to more positive resolutions.

Occasional reviews of our own philosophies can lead to a brighter and more enlightened journey.

Flint and Sparks

Burn those bridges!

A time or two, that was me in my younger years. I got angry at a few companies that did me wrong and let them know it. Spewing my anger in such a way, there was no "subject to interpretation" how I felt mistreated.

Fortunately I don't think it happened very often, but it did happen. When I look back now, I know that some of those instances occurred because I'd had so much stress on me financially that I couldn't have afforded the perceived injustice.

Somewhere along the way, I began to realize that firing strong statements at the other person only led them to feel called out and get defensive. They had no choice but to hold their ground. In the end, I often got burned.

Now, I can't say flinty feelings don't still occur at times due to life's challenges, but being older and wiser, my goal is often to sort through challenges with calm and patience. This means trying honestly to see things from the other party's point of view. It also requires thinking or writing what is to be said and then editing it until it sounds as neutral as possible before communication. By doing those two things, a great deal of the would-be sparks in life are reduced to minor dealings.

As you move forward each day, work to give problems no more value than they're truly worth. Ask yourself if, in a year, ten years, or long after you're gone, will the issue really be worth making a fuss about?

In more cases than not, problems that appear to deserve fireworks are resolved much easier without them.

Speeding Tickets

Most every person I know who has ever been pulled over by a police officer has an immediate sense of frustration and resentment toward the man or woman in blue. It might very well be human nature since the flashing light is a bit scary and it signals to the world we have just broken the law.

I must admit I have been pulled over, more than I care to admit. I can remember as a youth being agitated at the police officer, thinking he could be doing something better with his time than giving me a citation for speeding. Growing older I grudgingly realized that my lead foot had more to do with the flashing light than what side of the bed the police officer might have woken up on.

The truth of the matter is, I used to drive way too fast, way too often. Though I've been reluctant to admit it, the handful of instances I was given citations probably helped keep me from continuing to speed as time went on.

The guiding hand of authority is something most people need at some point in their life. It is only after such experiences that we actually appreciate that fact.

Shouldn't we each take account for who we are, where we are, and the circumstances we have placed ourselves in? In fact, every ticket I received for speeding has had one common thread—I was, in fact, speeding. As gray hairs have appeared on my head, I have accumulated the belief that there is more cause and effect in life than I used to give credit to.

These incidents of speeding tickets are merely a symbolism to life. The choices made often create the outcomes received. At the same time, wisdom of age has lent me understanding that the more one views themselves as the responsible party, the more power a person has over their own circumstances and the ability to change.

Personal responsibility is the true key to living life on our own terms.

If every person looked first in the mirror before casting a negative comment, thought, or action toward another person—in particular a person doing their job—we might make the world more pleasant for everyone. We might be the person that others want to be around more. We might also lift others up by setting the positive example.

As the days ahead unfold, may we each try to set a positive example, give a hand up, and brighten someone's day by our actions *and* responses. May you receive many happy returns for the good you bestow on others.

Power of Choice

Most of us have had books, of one kind or another, influence how we view the world around us. At times the people we encounter learn something from their reading and pass it along. In both instances the opportunity for education presents itself through the written word.

A very kind gentleman named William shared with me how he reads routinely and had picked up a book from the local library's recommended list. The book was the novel *The Last Days of Night*, set in 1888. It revolves around the inventors of electricity, including Thomas Edison, Nikola Tesla, and George Westinghouse. The incredible struggles for patents, power, and money were the basis for a story about these famous and wealthy men.

In addition to the overall interest he had in the book, one particular line stuck out to our patient. He said that in one section the author wrote about how rich people were different from the rest of us. The author wrote something to the effect that "such people could choose what they are miserable about." It was those words that had an impact on him.

He said that he did not have the means of a Westinghouse or Edison of their day. But he had the power each day to "choose what he was miserable about." While he sat with his friends at a coffee shop, his own mind began to think complaining thoughts, and he recalled the words.

In remembering, he realized he is rich. He is rich because he has a choice in deciding what he "can be miserable about." His wealth is in his freedom to choose.

Recalling the power of his own free will made him realize how fortunate he was. The power to choose meant he was fortunate and rich for being who he was, where he was, and in the situation he was. He was so grateful to be able to "choose what to be miserable about."

His insight provided a powerful lesson to me. Most of us have stress, resentment, frustration, or other negative emotions, which can balloon over time. It is the wise person who realizes there is a choice, and that choice is what makes us rich. This simple line from a book reveals the incredible freedom most every one of us have each day.

May we all find the path to making wise choices. This includes our state of mind. If the moment is ours to choose, we must be sure to choose wisely.

Psychology of a Victor

The people we meet often have wisdom accumulated through their life of experiences. Unfortunately, we do not always ask, and most do not provide guidance to us along our journey.

One of the people who has been willing to share, and whom I have trusted to give me advice, is Pastor Pullin. He is retired yet continues his ministry teaching a Sunday school class at his living community of Greencroft. He told me how one of the philosophies he taught twenty years ago has been something he still speaks of today, as he says, "with everyone who will listen."

What was it he found so valuable that he's compelled to keep sharing? It was this thought: "We always have a choice to make, and the choice we make always makes a difference."

He said the idea came from a statement he'd read from Victor Frankel, who had been a Jewish psychiatrist before he was taken to a Nazi death camp in World War II. He'd survived the incarceration by recognizing and living by the premise that he always had a choice, even if it was only to choose not to hate his captors.

Pastor Pullin shared the comment from Frankel, "Everything can be taken from a man but one thing: the last of the human freedoms—to choose one's attitude in any given set of circumstances, to choose one's own way."

I would certainly hope none of us are ever put in the circumstances of Victor Frankel, but we can likely learn something from his and Pastor Pullin's comments. It is a given that life will bring us many defeats, setbacks, betrayals, lies, and challenges to go along with hopefully equal or more positives. How we handle each situation has a lot more to do with who we are than the person or situation that caused the up or down.

Circumstances may be thrust upon us that we have limited to no control over, but many times the situations we find ourselves in are a result of our choices. Even the small choices we make every day factor into where we find our relationships, our social situations, and our finances.

The decisions we make at this moment help define our future, even if it is choosing our own peace from a given situation. These decisions can move us in the direction we most want to be.

Take the time to consider the choices you are making, and realize that choices do make a difference in our current and future situations.

Two Ears and One Moment

While on a trip with my daughter, I read a powerful passage in a book that changed my weekend. The passage read, "so hard to feel the stone and not the ripple."

The author described how there is always tension when a person is present (physically) but not really there (mentally). He shared how so many times we pretend to be in one place but are not actually there. This is because we may be sitting by right next to someone but our mind is somewhere else.

The distant place where we keep our thoughts partially focused prevents us from being wholly in the present for the person and situation we are truly in. Our mind's attempt to be in two places at once creates a tension that makes us stray from where we are.

On our way to the airport, my daughter shared how she'd ordered a new pair of shoes that were Christmas-themed. Her beam and delight in telling me about the purchase and the joy she would have when they arrived was wonderful to see. I only half caught it though. You can probably guess the reason.

My mind skipped away while she spoke, and then I asked when the shoes would arrive. Her reply was a blunt magnification of my failure to her. She said, "I just told you it would be three weeks." Since my mind had tried to hold two thoughts at once, I'd lost the trust and engagement I'd had with her during the drive. She knew I was only partially hearing what was said and my mind was engaged elsewhere.

I realized that the present moment (aka my daughter) deserved my full attention. It was one of those times I frequently long for where I would find the connection with my child who is growing up too fast. I lost the opportunity so quickly. To be trusted to hear the thoughts of my angel was more important than any stray wonder of my mind.

The small interaction served as a reminder of how easily one can lose the heart of others. At the same time, it reveals what is needed to keep the line of communication open.

Two ears and one mouth doesn't simply mean "talk less." It really means "listen more." Let the two ears guide the thoughts to *one* mind so we focus on the who and what that is important at the very moment we are in.

My lesson helped me be more attentive the rest of the weekend. The reward was a stronger connection with my angel.

May we each find the power of focus when we are with those we care dearly about. Our current moment is the most powerful and important we will have, for we only pass through it once.

Sweet Deal

At the age of ninety, a wonderful man in our practice shared how much he'd loved driving the Wakarusa school bus and helping children. I asked him how he got his start. That opened a window to the incredible person he was.

One of his first years driving, he'd had a group of children who were particularly rowdy—flat out hard to control and not wanting to listen to authority. He wasn't quite sure how to handle matters, but knew that he had to set the tone or else it would be one long year.

After having a "rules of the road" talk, he noticed some improvement. He also realized there might be a better way to achieve discipline than with a strong hand.

No one claimed the coins he found on the floor after the bus rides. His cup of coins grew, but even after announcements were made, nobody claimed them. Then he told the students the coins would be removed following week. Still no one stepped forward.

The following weekend, he took the cup of coins and bought lollipops—a favorite at the time. On Monday he had enough lollipops for every child. He explained the rules of the bus once again, and added that each child could have the treat if they followed the rules and picked up after themselves, leaving the bus as clean as they found it.

As one might imagine, the children followed every rule, picked up every wrapper, and enjoyed having the most wonderful bus driver they could have hoped for. He told me that the loose change count even increased a bit after this experiment.

His process of solving the rowdiness issue was more easily handled with a bit of sweet rather than the harsh edge of discipline.

How many times can a problem be solved by looking for the win-win in the situation? Finding what the other person wants or might find appealing may then open doors to success for both you and them—a truly sweet deal.

Consider the Source

If you are like me, your parents were the guiding forces for most of your early life. Interestingly, parents' views, habits, and tendencies often guide the decisions many children make well into adulthood. If you've ever thought, *Why did I do that?* a reason might be your upbringing.

In his best-selling book *The Road Less Traveled*, Dr. M. Scott Peck observed that many people look for acceptance or approval from their parents. For some, if that approval or acceptance doesn't come, they can be devastated. For others, they seem to overcome it. What is the difference?

Dr. Peck explained that many people don't realize parents are or were fallible humans just like us. What's more, parents' mistakes, challenges, and shortcomings can create a burden for the next generation.

He wrote that some people live in continual need of approval from others, often starting with their imperfect parents. However, once an individual realizes that all people are flawed humans who make judgements based on their own life experiences (and questionable responses to those experiences), they are able to realize something profound.

The discovery allows a person to become more self-reliant in their emotional needs, and not to rely on the errant emotions of others.

The next time we encounter someone who makes us feel bad, let's stop and ask ourselves why we feel this way. If we analyze the comment, keeping in mind that the source is imperfect, we can often keep a more positive outlook. Remember that you are important, and a good person. Remember that you and those around you have many more strong points than shortcomings.

Eavesdrop-worthy

Something said on television came to mind, reminding me how important each word we say can be. It came from a fellow who grew up a coach's son in a small town in Mississippi. As an adult, he was most often seen wearing blue jeans and a T-shirt. But on Sundays he wore a number 4 on his shirt and played quarterback for the Green Bay Packers. His name? Brett Favre.

During his Pro Football Hall of Fame induction speech, he recounted how, when he was a boy and his father a coach, they left for school early in the morning and stayed until his dad's work was done. With his dad being head coach, he was the last to turn out the lights.

Near the end of his high school years, Brett sat outside his father's office one night waiting to ride home. He heard his dad tell the other coaches, "I know he didn't play that well this week, but let me tell you men one thing. I know my son, and he will redeem himself next week." His father was talking about Brett.

During his induction speech, the quarterback also shared how his father's one moment of solid belief in him had helped carry him through a myriad of tough times to become one of the great football players of his generation.

It's amazing how impactful the right words at the right time, the right encouragement when it's needed, and the sharing of faith when entering the unknown, can be. In fact, the potential empowerment we gain from others can be life changing.

If you've ever felt positive thoughts about someone you care about and you believe in them, by all means, tell them so. It might not make them a Pro Football Hall of Fame quarterback, but it sure could fuel the special fire that burns inside them.

Give the words now, to them or to others about them, for secondhand praise can matter as much as firsthand. Let those who eavesdrop on you be encouraged.

Marble in the Pocket

As I have mentioned, I find there is so much to learn from reading the books of others. The lives and thoughts of those who have come before us can be exceptionally inspiring. Even if we gain but a small bit from authors when we read, over time a collection of these small changes can improve who we are as individuals.

A simple story I read in the book *You and Your Network* reminded me how we each have something of value to contribute to the world in our own way. At times we forget how much influence we have on the people in our lives, or we lack the confidence to realize our importance.

In this particular segment of the book, the author describes how a man twirled a marble in his hand while the two of them talked. He asked the gentlemen why he did that. The gentleman handed him the marble. It had a band around it with the Golden Rule inscribed.

He went on to explain how he'd had a great deal of trouble getting along with others until someone suggested that he work to make others feel important. The marble, he said, was his way to symbolize to him that whoever he talked to was important.

In reading this text, my thoughts took the principle a step further. I wondered how many people could make their own life better by first looking at themselves and evaluating why they are important, then remind themselves of this regularly. It's amazing how people in all walks of life seem to think of themselves as inferior in some area and discount how wonderful they truly are.

Each person in this world is unique. The fact is, no two people out of the more than seven billion on Earth have the exact same genetic makeup or the same environment that influences who we become.

If one then looks at the number of people we contact through the course of life and consider how many people each of those individuals contact, a perspective of importance can come into focus. The impact of one individual on the world around them is incredible.

Now, if we each had our own "marble" of sorts to remind us of the importance of who we are, the example we set for others, and the impact we have on the world, we might realize we are something *marvelous*. I would venture to say that if each person looked at their actions as influential to the people, circumstances, and events around them, our world would be a better and brighter place.

I hope this realization about yourself helps to make your surroundings better and brighter today.

Mr. Averill

Have you ever received a gift from someone that created a long-lasting impact? It can remind us the value is in the thought behind giving, and in the effect it has.

One of these gestures was made by a former teacher of mine to every student in his class. When students older than me found out I had Mr. Averill for my sixth-grade year, several asked if I had received the painting from him. They wouldn't tell me anything more. A bit of mystery and intrigue were stimulated.

Soon afterward, the teacher mentioned he would have a gift for us when he'd completed one for every student (well over a hundred kids that year).

On unveiling day he presented each student with the gift during a special ceremony. Each person received a cloth scroll bound by wooden ends. When I unfolded mine, a cheerful, bright orange- and yellow-themed painting of the sun filled a corner, and in the middle were scribed the words, "Never forget that Roger is a special person."

Our teacher had used a significant amount of detail and time. Looking back, the time he'd dedicated to create and personalize a scroll for every student seems even more daunting.

That gift was a fixture in my room for years after he presented it to me. Though he shared the same gift and the same words with other people, the personalized nature made it particularly compelling for me.

Today I think back and remember that a kind word and gift of hope and inspiration can be deeply meaningful. The words or gift might even be remembered for years after.

You never know when the kind words, inspirational thought, or gift you give might uplift another person. Such a kindness might have a positive influence for years to come.

Let's join together in spreading some sunshine on those around us today.

"Use the Force"

One of our patients shared with me that after he retired, his employer had called him back several times to see if he would resume work. I asked him a bit more about his job and why he'd been telephoned. I found myself impressed by his answers.

He was 81 years old when we talked, and 80 when he retired from delivering parts in a semitruck for Lippert Components. While working, he'd woken up at four in the morning, and he'd kept going until about five in the evening. His typical workweek had been 50 to 60 hours.

Though he said the job hadn't been difficult, it had required attention to detail, caution, and dependability. The steadiness in his eye and the pride in his voice made it evident he'd had a conviction to do his job well.

When he retired the company had tried multiple people to replace him but couldn't find the right fit. He told me, "I just feel I've had the commitment and work ethic that was needed."

His passion and words displayed the types of traits I find admirable. The commitment to excellence in one's chosen occupation, hobby, or pastime can produce extraordinary results and, as he described, it often fills a void.

He reminded me that no matter where we are or what we do, the opportunity to set high standards and go the extra mile is often a driving force within. When we unleash that force, the values of integrity, excellence, and dependability can be hard to replace.

It's wonderful to be part of a practice where people set a high standard of integrity for all of us. I am humbled to do what I do every day and appreciate the opportunity to be part of this community and our patients' lives.

Hunting Diamonds

A few years back, I read a story written by Russel Conwell called *Acres of Diamonds*. Mr. Conwell went on to become the first president of Temple University.

In the story, a farmer in a foreign country lived contentedly, until he decided he wanted to be very rich. After he learned of the possibility of diamonds being found on a certain type of land, his desire for wealth mushroomed. He sold his farm and went to search the world for the very kind of land where a diamond mine could be found to make him rich.

Sometime later, it was discovered that the very farmland the man had abandoned possessed dried-up riverbeds sprinkled with dark brown to black rocks. Upon investigation, the rocks were revealed to be diamonds.

The place right where he had stood had contained his riches all along.

The parable reminds us that the best place to find success is often right where we're at. The people we know, the skills we have, the knowledge we've gained, and so much more might very well make us best suited for success right here, right now. At the same time, to achieve success we may need to seek out fresh possibilities and determine how we can best take advantage of our current situation.

One might also consider the fact that riches in life might very well be the health, happiness, and relationships we have, or can have, where we are.

As in the parable, may you find the acres of diamonds in your own life. And may they brilliantly shine.

Up on a Rooftop

Sleeping on the roof was about the strangest thing I'd ever heard of. This was especially the case when it was told to me about my father.

My father died quite a while ago. Long after his death, one my relatives told me some of his experiences. According to the relative, my father's family of origin didn't have much in terms of material wealth, so he was one of eleven children raised in the poorest part of town. Somehow the meager means didn't seem to limit him, like I think it might have limited myself. This was no better demonstrated than the year my father as a young man attended college.

After commuting between home and college the spring semester, he had the opportunity to work but felt he still couldn't afford rent in the autumn.

So what did he and his friend do? The two college boys set up cots on the roof of the dorms. They would sleep under the stars, drop down in the morning to shower, then head off to class or work.

I'm not sure how long this occurred, but it sure seems brazen to me. My father was not the type to speak much, and since he's passed away I will never know the details of this curious escapade.

Somewhere in his life of poverty he learned to be self-sufficient. At the same time, he became a humanitarian in his own way. He once shared with me how it was the right thing to do to help others, create friendships, and make sure your partners in life dealings got the better end of the deal.

I can also remember him telling me, "No one is better than you, and you are no better than anyone." He shared how we should treat each person with great respect and not be intimidated by the social class or standing of another person because, as he would say, "We all put our pants on one leg at a time."

Though I may not sleep on roofs, I must say I appreciate the lessons he taught. The paths of those who go before us can help light the way of our own destinies.

Take time to get to really know the people in your life. May you enjoy much enlightenment.

Marshmallow Gratification

If you ever had a fireside marshmallow as a child, the memory might allow your five senses to reexperience the dark, crispy surface and smooth, soft inside of the warm, tasty delight. If we think about it for a bit, many of us can conjure up a few nice memories to go along with our roasted marshmallows.

Walter Mischel wrote the book *The Marshmallow Test*, which detailed some of his research on children and marshmallows while he was at Stanford University. He and his team placed each child in a room with a marshmallow, and then tested various parameters. An example might be telling the child that if they waited until the researcher returned, they would get two marshmallows rather than the one in front of them.

With different factors and times given for the children, their responses were recorded. Over a period of years the data was observed, and interpretations were able to be made.

What Mr. Mischel did was watch a person's ability to use "delayed gratification," starting at an early age. His research found that children who could employ delayed gratification performed better in school, including on SAT scores.

The really cool part of his research, though, was that it revealed people, including adults, can learn delayed gratification. Whether trying to eat healthy, quit smoking, or simply improve our life, focusing on the long-term benefits rather than the satisfaction of the moment can help overcome dependency.

If we can practice overcoming short-term impulse urges, we can become better at handling our long-term goals.

May we each find the power in ourselves to improve our future. Try cutting back just one bad habit (skip one cookie/cake/pie) each day this week, and you are depositing power into a bank of self-control. Before long, your bank will be one you can be truly proud of.

Outside In

A fellow classified as a motivational speaker, Jim Rohn, once shared a story that has stuck with me. It was about effect—the effect of doing good for others and the world around you.

He described thinking back to times his mother had told him not to throw his candy wrappers on the ground but take them to the trash. As a child he wondered why that one little piece of trash would make any difference to another human or to the world around him. From his youth he could not figure out why she was so adamant about him doing right, even with the smallest of things like candy wrappers.

He said as he got older he began to understand. He would think of her as he left his hotel room and had to decide whether to leave the lights on or turn them off.

Mr. Rohn realized the right decision was not the one requiring least effort, but the right thing to do for the world he lived in. And if more people made those small decisions, the impact could be large on the global stage.

Elaborating, Mr. Rohn stated that a person should do good for others and for the world around them, not only for the betterment of the world, but do it also for the effect it has on the person doing the action.

He explained the pattern of actions an individual takes can shape a person inwardly, and help them elevate the way that person thinks of him or herself. Somebody doing even little things to make the world a better place is becoming a person of more significance, and confidence. Thus, the small steps we take make a difference in who we are.

If we all add a few more good deeds to our activities, regardless of how small, the world will be a better place. Whether it is a kind word to the grocery clerk, picking up a piece of trash we didn't leave behind, or helping a neighbor without being asked, some small step can make an important difference.

The difference might very well be in us.

Surprises

They say in giving gifts "It's the thought that counts." I am a bit embarrassed to say that when I was young, the gift mattered more than it should have. As I have grown older, the effort a person puts in holds greater value.

The best example for me was on a birthday when my two high-school daughters created a pretty special evening. My wife told me to make sure I was home at a reasonable time after work. I arrived at the house to find my daughters had cooked dinner and also made a birthday cake. It was so special to have them take the time and be so thoughtful to make a special evening for me. I could not have been more appreciative.

After dinner the girls huddled around and whispered, "Should we take him now?" Storm clouds were rolling in, and the sky was darkening. The girls expanded their secret and plainly told me, "We want to take you for a ride in the golf cart."

We had purchased a rugged, ten-year-old golf cart the prior year, and the girls loved tootling around our place with it. This evening they loaded me on to take me on a tour of our yard.

As we toured I saw that my oldest daughter had purchased plastic and metal recycled artwork shaped as flowers and the sun. She had strategically placed these as well as balloons along a path around the property.

With the oldest in the driver's seat, they drove me around with both girls beaming so bright with pride and delight it infected me too. You could not have wiped the smile off my face that night. The fact they had done so much for my special day made me well up.

It is truly amazing when someone shares their heart to make your day better.

Sometimes our children teach us lessons in life. This display of caring and effort will be a lifetime memory for me. It'll also remind me that "it really is the thought that counts."

As we move forward in our own life, may we each find the time to help create a positive memory for someone we care about. It may not be the cost, but the thought, that genuinely makes the moment special.

Doing something nice, especially when unexpected, can create a moment to cherish for a lifetime. If each of us did this from time to time for someone we care about, the world we live in would be a happier place. We would also likely find that the deed adds fulfillment to our own life, greater than we might expect.

Drumroll, Please

Do you recall a time when you felt forced to do something? Whether at work, school, or at home this is often when we feel like we have no choice. Some people debate the notion that there is "no choice," but for the most part there are situations in which we simply can't stand the alternative.

One time in sixth grade, I asked if I could drop out of band and take a different class. You see, I had chosen a drum as my instrument, and three days a week I had to lug this huge drum-sized plastic case on the bus to school, through the hallways, and back home. Then when I arrived at practice, the other drummer was so good I simply felt stupid because this was my first year playing.

Asking for an option out seemed like the simple, easy fix. My reasoning was good, from my vantage point, since no one could disagree with long bus rides lugging the drum and its case . . . or with having a loss of desire, and not being very good.

My father was willing to meet with the principal to discuss it. To my dismay (and somewhat to my father's), Mr. James, our principal, said the move was not an option. Once I'd signed up at the start of the year, he said, the commitment had been made. There was no negotiation, and thus no change.

Though I was hurt and angry at Mr. James for not letting me opt out, the situation taught me something valuable: When you commit to a thing, expect to follow through. From that point on, I knew if a commitment was being made then I must complete the task.

The principal's stern response hadn't been what I'd wanted to hear, but it had helped me dig with more devotion into things I did want to do, from that day on.

It's sometimes the people giving us the perceived "short end of the stick" who help push us to develop traits or skills that make us stronger for the future. It is through experiences and pains that we grow.

If ever you or someone you care about gets the "short end of the stick," remember that traits learned from the experience might better equip a person for the future. So, if you're handed that stick, roll up your sleeves and, to the best of your ability, drum on through it.

Look Ahead

You might recall one of my favorite sayings, "The best time to plant a tree was twenty years ago. The second-best time is now." That thought blended well with the late Paul Meyer's philosophy that we should plan and build for the long haul.

Mr. Meyer explained that each time he bought a home, he planted trees, painted fences, and fixed all the problems he could see. His said he always worked to build up the places he lived so that whoever owned the properties in the future would be pleased the work was done.

The "long-haul" approach led to decisions being made that removed the "quick-fix" mentality. Though some delayed gratification was required, the end result proved worth it.

This approach can certainly add beauty and value to a home, even though effort is taken to make it possible.

If we expand the "plan and build" philosophy to our social life, it might help us be more involved in our community, take the time to be a friend others are glad to have, and put forth efforts that lead to more meaningful experiences. Over time, we may very well have more true friends and make a significant difference in the area of the world we live in.

Furthermore, using this philosophy at work may show our bosses we are the type of people who can grow into greater responsibility and bigger roles.

In essence Mr. Meyer appears to encourage us to take responsibility for who we are and where we are by building the best world around us. If we happen to outgrow our current circumstance, then at the very least we'll leave behind a better place than the one we started with.

More Than Skin Deep

What happened to President Jimmy Carter?

Former President Carter was diagnosed with metastatic melanoma in May 2015. This cancer usually starts in a mole on the skin and is the reason dermatologists implore each person to check their skin each month. If anything suspicious is found, a dermatology visit is needed right away.

His melanoma aside, a fascinating aspect about President Carter is his genuine concern for others. He has helped Habitat for Humanity grow by incredible bounds. He couldn't do this without the wonderful help of many people, including a variety of those in most every community. I cannot count the number of people who have told me they've volunteered with Habitat for Humanity. I commend each person who helps with this and any venture that lends a hand to the less fortunate.

This same mind-set facilitates our own community's growth.

After he retired, one kind man from our community used his skills in business and construction by going to Georgia to assist Habitat for Humanity. Though his role was small at first, his willingness to dedicate time, experience, and his ability to manage made him a key person to manage important projects with Habitat for Humanity.

During his years of service, he caught the eye of the former president, who then became acquainted with him. President Carter even personally asked this local man to handle a few of the larger projects he had underway.

Through his work and time spent with President and Mrs. Carter, a bond formed between the families. A friendship grew to the point that the president even had our local gentleman and his wife over to his home for Thanksgiving dinner one year.

The work he did was so important to President Carter that he gave this local man a wooden piece of furniture that the president had made. It has been the president's custom to make one piece each year and sell it, with proceeds going to charity. For this particular year, instead of selling it for charity, the president gave the piece to our local friend as a gesture of gratitude for the incredible work he had done through his many years of service to Habitat.

After giving thought to the impact that the money this handmade piece of furniture sold might have on others if it were auctioned off, our local man asked if it would be acceptable for the president to take it back and sell it like he had the other wooden pieces he'd made. The president agreed, and the item was sold for more than $100,000.

Though many of us will not get to meet a president through our volunteer efforts, we can make a significant difference for many. May we find it in our hearts to give a hand up when we have the opportunity. Though we might not save the world, the ones we may save could then make a difference in the lives of others.

(Note: Early detection is crucial for melanoma survival. It is important to know what to look for and to have it removed before it spreads. Melanoma is one of the key reasons to see a dermatologist each year. Along with your appointment, we offer a free complimentary skin cancer educational guide. My team and I would be honored to see you and perform your skin cancer screening. Call our office today.)

Quick to Listen, Slow to Speak

Have you ever felt helpless and wished you could do more? Well I certainly have, more times than I want to count. One time in particular wasn't long ago, when my aunt called and asked me for advice while her husband (my uncle) lay on his death bed.

The previous day they had taken a walk and sat down to admire the flowers along a hiking trail near their RV. It was the type of peaceful day they had planned for in their retirement, which was just around the corner for my uncle, nearing age seventy. You see, he had decided to take fewer jobs around the country in his management role so that he could spend time with my aunt.

The evening of the walk, he stood on a stepladder to fix the awning on the RV. The ladder slipped out from under him, and he fell and hit his head.

My aunt called me the next day. The doctors caring for my uncle had determined his fall would eventually be fatal due to brain damage. She needed to decide if it was time to withdraw care and let him die, or carry on without any hope of a meaningful recovery.

The question of when to stop care required an answer I wasn't sure how to provide.

Only later did it dawn on me that what she had really been looking for hadn't been an answer at all. My aunt had already known the decision she had to make, and she'd called the only medical person in her family to be sure she was making the right one. She'd simply needed support outside of her own sons to finalize the decision.

As I look back on my memories of the event, I can't help but wonder if I could have handled it better for her. What else might I have done? The rational part of me knows that people in times of crisis need one thing first and foremost, and that is an ear to listen—an ear without judgement, without a mouth, and without a quick retort.

It's not the ability to solve, but rather the willingness to listen that can make a profound impact.

May we each find a way to lend our ear to those around us a bit more this week. You never know when it might create clarity for those we are listening to.

Make Home Movies

After my uncle passed away, I couldn't get certain thoughts about it out of my mind.

The day before he died, he and my aunt had been on an RV trip. They had taken a walk and sat down to admire the flowers along a hiking trail near where they'd parked. My aunt shared with me that this had been a perfect little spot to rest on a sunny day, a place where they had enjoyed several moments of tranquility. As she described it to me, she painted the setting of beautiful green grass and colorful flowers. It was the type of day my aunt and uncle had planned for in their retirement.

The evening of the walk, my uncle had stood on a stepladder to fix the awning on the RV. The ladder had slipped out from under him, and he'd fallen and hit his head. He'd been taken to the hospital and in a short time had passed away.

I sometimes think about what wonderful people each of them had always been, and how well they'd raised their own children. But the main thought that keeps recurring is that I am so glad my aunt can look back to the day before he died, knowing they'd shared peace and the wonders of nature together right before he left us. What a blessing to have left his wife in such a positive frame of mind.

We often experience similar events, which cause us to reflect on how fleeting life can be. Wouldn't it be wonderful if each day we left those around us with uplifting mental "video clips" of the moments they were last in our presence? These little experiences can be remembered by the loved ones we'll leave behind someday. If we realize that over time those video clips can become strong, vibrant memories, we understand that we just might be creating a wonderful "home movie" of unforgettable moments that will replay in our family's and friends' hearts year after year.

Go make some memories today worthy of becoming unforgettable mental video clips. Know that the smallest, kindest, and gentlest moments might be the most meaningful.

Unexpected Gift

The saying "behind every good man is a great woman" had an outstanding example at Indiana University.

Coach Hoeppner's wife, Jane, went through multiple moves as a coach's wife, supporting him on his career path to become head coach. Each move she hoped it would be the last, while also knowing that, in the coaching profession, her dream wasn't likely to become a reality.

Finally her husband landed a head coaching job. His passion for football was second only to his passion for mentoring young boys to grow into men of integrity. Though the players and many in the community bought into his vision, it was cut short by his untimely brain tumor diagnosis. Coach Hoeppner had terminal cancer. He passed away.

Afterward, his wife shared how her identity was lost. She wasn't sure what to do. One year after her husband's death, on the eve of the first home game, she received a knock on her door. As she opened the door, a delivery of flowers awaited her, along with a note from one of her husband's former players. The note held a saying her husband had spoken to his players many times: "Never ever quit."

She was shocked but also felt a warmth of calm, as though the coach personally touched her that day.

We can only imagine the emotions she has gone through in her process of grieving, but it's incredible to see that the teachings of her husband lived on to influence her life after his passing.

His football victories pale in comparison to the impact he had on those around him. And Jane was the great woman who had supported his efforts and career. It was Jane's hope in writing her book, *Never Ever Quit*, that her husband's example would help us better the world beyond our reach and after we are gone.

If we, like her, never ever quit, will that not be one of our life's greatest achievements?

Notre Dame Press Box

A retired sport telegrapher met *who*? Well, that was a fun story a pleasant man shared with me. He'd worked for Western Union typing on a telex machine—a typewriter-like unit linked through a network to send rapid messages. His job had been to sit in the Notre Dame press box and type what was happening at the football games.

Accuracy was a primary expectation of his job. This became frustrating the night his arm got bumped while USC was playing with O. J. Simpson in the backfield.

The press box was packed with VIPs. Even Bob Hope sat down the way from him enjoying the game. So he'd expected a tight fit, but his job was important. Then he was bumped again.

He glanced up. He thought he knew the fellow but couldn't place him. He resumed his work.

At a time out, the telegrapher turned to see who had bumped him. A hand was extended toward him, followed by a big smile. The fellow said, "Hi, I'm Jim Nabors. Sorry I bumped you there."

He said Mr. Nabors was quite friendly and asked about his work and complimented him as well.

It was enjoyable to hear him recall his encounter with the famous man who, from 1972 until 2014, had sung at the start of the Indianapolis 500, and had been part of *The Andy Griffith Show* playing Gomer Pyle.

If we each pretended a famous person was the one who did us wrong when we get bumped into, cut off in traffic, or cut in front of, maybe we might not let it get to us so much. So the next time you feel jolted a bit, ask yourself what you would do if Jim Nabors was the one knocking you off track. You never know when you might receive the bright smile of a good person offering an apology for an unintentional wrong.

Pennies in the Bank

From a young age I was taught to put pennies in the bank. I can remember as I grew up a local soda manufacturing company would provide children at social events soda cans with a slot in the top to put money in. Those cans, along with our regular piggy banks, were so fun filling up and taught me valuable lessons.

Now as an adult I look back and ask myself if there is a parable in life to the little piggy bank. And I think there is. In looking at how things unfold, I realize that "pennies in the bank" are good to have but not anywhere near as powerful as the principle being taught. The concept is building up a full bank through placing many deposits of what we are saving on multiple occasions.

As a dermatologist I see so many people with skin problems who have spent a great deal of time in the sun through their youth and even adult life. Some come in during those first twenty to forty years of life for one reason or another. After walking out of a room for someone who is here for acne or warts and proclaims they are not worried about their current and past suntanning, I walk right into the next room with a different patient deeply concerned about the effects sun has had on their skin. Whether wrinkles, brown spots, or skin cancer, the sun contributes to many skin problems.

In looking at this vast difference in these two populations, I can't help but draw an analogy to the "pennies in the bank" childhood practice. The person who has sun damage often spent years with too much sun, but only when a threshold of age, sun damage, and genetics all mesh do they find an unpleasant result. In looking back, most of them recognize that their actions at least in some degree contributed to the end result.

Life may not always be fair or just, but there is often a correlation between our actions and the results we get. It may not seem so at the time, but many of life's big problems come from errors in judgement repeated every day. The sooner we realize we control so much of our current day—and this then means we control much of our future—the sooner we gain independence and/or control.

We can begin figuratively filling our piggy banks by the steps we take right now. Whether it is better health, better relationships, or better financial outcomes, may we each begin the small steps today of putting "pennies in our bank" for a better tomorrow.

As we move forward from today, may you find the power to make small decisions that will leverage to a brighter future.

With Wit Like This

One of our patients has been carrying the diagnosis of ALS. The letters ALS stand for amyotrophic lateral sclerosis, which is also called Lou Gehrig's disease.

Our patient came in for treatment of a skin cancer on his left forearm. During our conversation he mentioned how ALS usually took months to years to overcome all normal functioning. He said his had been slow, until the previous month when he was reduced to a wheelchair.

Rather than hunt for pity, he described how he looked for all the positives he could find. He remained grateful for seventy-four years on this earth. He was proud of his decades-long marriage. He chided his friends and invited them to pick on him in return.

After he threw that gauntlet, one of his friends told him he might get slapped after he dies, just to make sure he wasn't alive. Another friend said he'd turn him upside down after he passed away and use him for a bike rack.

Our patient's humor remained rapier sharp. He told me that a friend of his recently passed away, and his grandchildren had lined up to put money inside his casket for fishing lures, dinner out, and all sorts of crazy items. When it was his turn to approach his friend's casket, our patient eyed all the money sitting there in front of him. He reached into his pocket, pulled out something, and started writing on it. His wife then noticed he was dropping his hand alongside a fifty-dollar bill in the casket. She grabbed his hand and asked what he was doing. He told her, "I'm not stealing anything. I'm swapping out the cash for this check."

Though most of us will never be diagnosed with something as devastating as this patient has, I hope we remember how invaluable a sense of humor is in our everyday life. Besides being scientifically proven to reduce stress, aid in healing illness, and facilitate stronger relationships, a good chuckle can keep life's troubles in perspective.

May you and I find the courage to handle challenges by focusing on the positive. And when we feel like crying, may we take a moment to smile and laugh at life, as it may help to lighten the load.

Truly Tech

It's always a pleasure to share time with you, whether in the office or through technology. The sheer amazement I feel for the advances in our high-tech world is vast. Each day something new and better is created.

While teaching and mentoring Indiana University medical students, it's always fun to learn what they know and watch how they perform. One of my fourth-year medical students followed me on rounds, toting along some electronic device a bit larger than a phone. He kept looking down at it and appeared to almost ignore the conversations I had with several patients. Time and time again, I saw him look down at his apparatus, tap the screen, and stare off into the mysteries of the device.

I tried not to pry, though this went on for most of the morning. Then, after an unusual diagnosis, he leaned over as we left the examination room and said, "That was really cool. I'm glad I can look up what you're talking about right here (pointing to his device) while we're in the room. It helps me learn so much faster."

Who would have thought? Here I was thinking he wasn't enjoying his rotation or paying much attention. As it turns out, he was fascinated with it all. He actually found dermatology a delight, and what he saw and heard he looked up on his iPad-like device.

This little experience reminded me of two things. One is we shouldn't pass judgement on others, since we aren't always accurate in our thinking. The second is we might as well embrace technology. It truly can enhance the world we live and work in.

La Critique

Have you ever been around someone who is quite critical? The criticism one flings around can be hurtful. Often the person flinging it doesn't even realize what they're doing. I know a bit about this, since I used to be way too critical, and unfortunately at times have been known to fall back into that role.

What many criticizers or reformed criticizers don't understand is that the practice of criticism is really passing judgement. This means a person is constantly evaluating things as right or wrong, good or bad.

Unbeknownst to the person who hasn't learned to move beyond this behavior is that the process creates a continual cycle of turbulence in their own internal dialogue. This then constricts a person's ability to fulfill their potential in other areas and see things in a more open light.

On the other hand, nonjudgement, as a practice, can allow a person's day to flow more smoothly. Even if it's for a few hours, the process of avoiding judgement allows a person to see the world for what it is rather than an interpretation of the rights or wrongs within it. This allows the unfettered, fluid nature of life to occur as it is often meant to be.

The results can include a reduction in fear, insecurity, and feelings of superiority, which often live inside the critical person's mind.

When we suspend our criticism, doors to opportunities can be opened, including those we never knew existed. If we can wait a day before passing judgement at home, work, or at social events, we may very well find the people around us are much easier to work with.

If you feel the need to tell someone how or what to do, hold on to the thought a day or so and see if the best thing might be to just let it go. Positive support can help foster and grow, while a harsh word can do more harm than we know.

Golfer's Resolve

What if you woke up one morning and couldn't remember who you were and where you were at?

This actually happened to one of our patients. While golfing on the golf course that he had designed and owned, he told his friends he didn't feel well and then collapsed. Since his home bordered the course, he was helped back to his house. He felt like his condition wasn't serious and stayed home for another two days.

Then he was taken to the hospital, unconscious. There doctors found an aneurysm. The aneurysm caused him to remain in the hospital. It was not known if he would live. But he did live.

When he regained consciousness, he had no memory of his family, including his wife, and he'd forgotten important life skills, most notably the ability to read.

It took weeks before he learned who his wife was. After six months in a rehab facility, he was discharged home, still with a very limited memory and limited skills. His health care team told him he shouldn't expect much more, if any, improvement.

Well, he and his wife never gave up. And after fifteen years, he finally developed the ability to read again.

The dedication he and his wife showed to his recovery was nothing short of amazing. His tenacity and willingness to fight on was matched only by the commitment of his wife. Together they worked and challenged him to regain as much normal functioning as possible.

Though most people will never face this challenge, each of us can learn from them.

Do not quit, no matter how hard things may seem. Do not give in to naysayers who tell you something "can't" be done. And always expect to improve, regardless of your circumstances.

You are destined to overcome, and will do so, despite your current situation, if you first resolve to move forward.

Give Out to Fill Up

How many times have you been told, "It's better to give than receive"? If you're like me, you've wondered what in the world that really means. So let's dig deeper.

Well, what does it mean to give? Some feel it is the parting of money. To others it's passing on what is more than they need. Yet others feel it is the giving within a relationship to another person.

From the dictionary it is all of these—it's transferring something you possess, whether material or immaterial, to someone else.

So why is it better to give? Some believe it is because the more you give, the more you receive, whether the gift is material (sharing extra household goods) or immaterial (volunteering time to help a friend or acquaintance). This occurs because gifts multiply when given, just as seeds can only multiply if planted. Other people see giving as a method to pave the way to good opportunities. Still others feel it brings peace to the giver, as if giving were a sprout that can grow a tall tree of goodness.

The truth is, each person has to determine what this saying means to them.

Though I don't propose to know the answer, I know giving has helped me feel better inside. The intention to give and the follow-through often act like pennies deposited in a piggy bank inside my heart. The more deposited, the stronger my gratefulness for the things I have.

Though there may be no one explanation for the saying, the older I become the more clearly the saying seems to indicate that the giver gains. When we think of others, the good comes back to us.

Explore for yourself why giving is better than receiving. I am certain you won't be disappointed.

When Holding a Shield Strengthens the Arm

The troubles and life struggles each person goes through is often hidden behind a shield the person has built in order to get through their life the best way they know how. This power of others amazes me every day.

During a surgery visit, a most pleasant eighty-eight-year-old man shared a bit of his life. His father had left him and his mother when he was very young, and his mother had remarried a man with a child of his own. This created a great deal of stress for a boy who was only five.

The stepfather was harsh with his words and strict to the point it left our patient a bit withdrawn around others. He recalled how the stepfather had always introduced him to others as "the boy I'm raising." Though the stepfather was religious by his actions, he left his stepson lacking the emotional support a child longs for.

Our patient shared that the way he was treated made it hard to be outgoing. He felt something was lacking in his life.

He recalled how he got up to speak in front of the class for a book report assignment, and he simply could not do it. The female teacher, who'd actually taught his mother years earlier, had kindly led him to a back coat closet, closed the door, and, after sitting supportively in front of him, said gently, "Now tell me that book report." His report in this environment was fantastic, and he passed his English class in part due to her understanding and caring way.

Our patient, at eighty-eight, now leads his church congregation in singing each Sunday. He enjoys his role so much he also leads Sunday evening and Wednesday evening songs. He has come a long way from the shy boy who was so insecure he could not stand in front of his classmates. At his current age, he can see that how he was raised had an effect on him most of his life.

When I asked him about his own children, twinkles in his eyes became evident as he said, "Love from me is not something my children lacked for."

His struggles in early life and the related insecurities have likely been hidden from most everyone he has encountered. His uncommon openness at this age reminded me how every person has experiences and challenges that shape and mold who they are. Unfortunately, some of the hidden challenges and negative occurrences are kept bottled up.

Though life is not fair, I hope each of us can take a moment for those we interact with and realize they might need a bit more understanding, a touch of empathy, or a helping hand. And if you are going through a rough spell, I hope you can find the support you need to rise above and triumph through your difficulty. You, like our patient, just might be making changes in the next generation with your actions.

Strong Foundation

My thoughts tuned in as the radio announcer discussed a new foundation near our practice in Elkhart. The foundation was designed to help children in local schools get items they may not otherwise have access to. This included everything from school supplies all the way to sanitary supplies. If basic needs are not met, the announcer pointed out, how can we expect a child to succeed?

The radio spot noted that it's not uncommon for teachers to spend up to $1000 per year of their own money to get supplies for their classrooms. Then the announcer requested donations from listeners so the foundation could give to schools for the kids.

The mention of $1000 per year amazed me. This became especially outstanding when a wonderful retired educator in our practice told me how many years his pay rate had either been held the same or only slightly increased.

It's astonishing the dedication teachers make giving a positive example and a helping hand.

Commitment to the youth of tomorrow truly makes the world a better place. So many of our educators in this country are helping day after day make positive impressions on children who need guidance and inspiration. For some, the inspiration they receive at school may be the only place they get a loving and caring hand.

Though many teachers have told me they could very well have made more economically by using their skills in another career field, the satisfaction of helping develop children is what moves them each day.

Join me in passing along a "thank you!" to educators, current and past, who have made a life out of improving our future.

And for all who have made a point to help another person, be proud of the difference you make in our world. Thank you.

Harmonica Man

It's fun to share about some of the fantastic people I have met. One such man, at the ripe age of ninety, told me the means by which he continues to give back.

As a self-taught harmonica player, he found a way to play for others as often as he could. He and his wife, who played the piano, shared their musical gift with those at the Greencroft Healthcare retirement community until her dementia was too severe.

With his passion still intact, he teamed up with a partner who played the guitar, who, by the way, was ninety-nine. The two of them played four days a week for half an hour per session.

He shared with me how the listeners livened up the moment the tunes began. Smiles spread across the room, feet tapped, and bodies moved.

When I asked if they played the same tunes each week, he said, "We have a big list of songs to choose from, and we try to mix it up. The people we play for don't remember what we played the week before, and I know at our ages, we don't either."

The music, he said, was something beautiful since many in their older years start losing the ability to recall lyrics, but the harmony of music remains intact. He also mentioned how the human connection is powerful at his gigs, and when he leaves he gives out abundant hugs, which are shared in joy.

His demonstration of commitment, caring nature, and good spirit are an inspiration. May his deeds shine a light to lead us all to be a bit more giving in our days to come. We might just be paying it forward . . . or in his case, paying it backward.

Bob Hope and 007

Have you ever heard the term *connector*?
Malcolm Gladwell, in his best-selling book *Tipping Point*, used this term. He described how some people know quite a few other people, and they are in the position to introduce acquaintances for business and other advantageous reasons. It seemed we are each potentially closer to many others in the world than we might realize.

After learning about this, I started looking at some of the connections we've had through people in our practice. I found it fascinating to think about. We had a retired Indiana Hall of Fame announcer share how his start in broadcasting had involved time working under the famous Kentucky basketball coach Adolph Rupp. Another of our clients was a sports telegrapher who was working in the Notre Dame press box at a game where Bob Hope and Jim Nabors were present.

In retirement one couple volunteered at Habitat for Humanity and eventually became good friends with former President Jimmy Carter and his wife. Also there was a woman who met Hilary Clinton after her grandson married the child of Ms. Clinton's former college roommate.

We even had a gentleman who went on a date with a Bond Girl from the old James Bond movie series that featured 007 played by actor Roger Moore.

To add to the history of our country, one client was a businessman. While at a dinner business meeting in Boston, one of the Boston business members coaxed a man in attendance to share who his relative was. It turned out the man, named Mr. Key, was the grandson of none other than Francis Scott Key, who wrote the "Star Spangled Banner."

It has been fun to explore and think about some of the connections we have within our dermatology family. And, more importantly, it reminds me how we are tied together in so many ways, often more than we realize.

In understanding how closely each of us in this world truly is to each other, it would seem we are meant to work together. Let's do our part to make our world a better place, as we never know who we are connecting with.

May you and your loved ones find a world willing to work with you for causes greater than any one of us can accomplish alone.

Legacy

If you have ever met a person who is at true peace, the experience can be powerful. This happened to me and two of our medical assistants during one of our visits.

A wonderful woman we had seen for years came in and told us she would not be scheduling her six-month follow-up appointment. She looked great and emitted a glow that brightened the room. Her presence was one that made me want to be around her. It's hard to describe, but her aura exuded love, compassion, and peace. The sparkle in her eyes and smile on her face beckoned the same feeling in return.

When I asked her why she was not making her next appointment, she said it was because she had been diagnosed with pancreatic cancer of the most severe kind. She went on to describe that she felt well today, but she was told her disease had spread and she would not live more than three to six months. As I offered condolences, she thanked me and then proceeded to share why she was so calm.

The first thing she mentioned was that she had been able to spend a great deal of time with her grandchildren in the last few years. She then described how fortunate she felt that her family was strong and close. And lastly, she felt strong in her faith and said she was ready to accept whatever her future would bring. She mentioned she had lived a life with many blessings.

The calmness, contentment, and peace she exuded was truly amazing. I found myself wondering how she had gotten to that point. Her image lives on in me as an aspiration. The strength to know we have given our best to this life and the contentment in knowing we have left nothing undone is awesome.

In looking back at her visit with us, I remember that she'd said the important facts were time with family, having good relationships with those she cared about, and being grounded in her faith. Family, relationships, and faith sound like her take-home message. The placement of these had allowed her to exude peace in the most trying of circumstances.

Though we may not all have the calmness she displayed in her situation, I would venture to say making the best of our family, friendships, and faith is sound advice. Giving a bit more effort to each may very well bring us peace during our final days.

About the Author

Dr. Roger T. Moore was raised in the small town of Elida (population 181), New Mexico, and later moved thirty miles to the big city of Portales (population 11,850). He grew up working on the family's farm and ranch, spending summers building fence, feeding and tending cattle, and driving tractors. Most summers he worked for his mother's father, Temple Rogers (who he was named after—Roger Temple Moore). His father often told young Roger that if he turned out like his grandfather he would be just fine. This grandfather was someone Roger always admired, looked up to, and emulated. Temple was regarded as the hardest working man in his town, an honest person of integrity, and a fellow who was a straight shooter.

Though neither of Roger's parents graduated college, each put incredible effort into him being able to reach his dreams. He feels he grew up as a most fortunate child because his mother, Annelle, and his father, Dick, made so much of his life possible.

Dr. Moore's initial passion in life was football, and he walked on at Texas Tech University for one year. After two surgeries on his knee, he returned home to the college in his hometown, Eastern New Mexico University. There he played linebacker for a conference champion team, until another knee surgery ended his playing career. The upbeat attitude and demeanor of his orthopedic surgeon, Dr. Bill Barnhill (a US Ski Team physician), inspired the recently injured Roger to become an orthopedic surgeon.

So Roger changed his major from marketing to pre-med his junior year of college, threw his heart into his studies, and set out to become a doctor. Changing areas of study so late in his college career required an inordinate amount of study. Dr. Moore attributes the work ethic his family instilled in him on the farm for giving him the wherewithal to make this change and climb the mountain of work ahead of him. The effort paid off—he gained entrance into four medical schools. He chose Texas Tech University Medical School, where he graduated near the top of his class, earning induction into the prestigious Alpha Omega Alpha honor society.

Entering his medical school training, Roger knew he loved surgery and the immediate results a patient received. Orthopedics was his desire. What he soon found out, though, was that he enjoyed getting to know patients and continuing his relationships with them even more. His heart was torn between following his mentor's path of orthopedics or finding an alternative career.

Fortunately and unfortunately, his father had squamous cell carcinoma of the lower lip before Roger entered medical school and had suggested dermatology as a career path. Roger researched this field and found that as a dermatologist he would perform procedures and surgeries, which gave him the satisfaction of cure and immediate results. At the same time, this area of medicine allowed him to maintain continuity of care with his patients, since many dermatology patients came in regularly for skin checkups. This would allow Dr. Moore to get to know his patients and continue caring for them over long periods of time. A perfect mesh was found.

Dr. Moore was able to gain entrance into the prestigious Rush-Presbyterian-St. Luke's Medical Center for his dermatology residency. There he worked with some of the iconic dermatologists of the modern era, including Dr. Arthur Rhodes (one of, if not the, leading mole guru of our time), Chairman Dr. Michael Tharp (an internationally recognized dermatologist for his work on hives and urticaria), Dr. Marianne O'Donoghue (an integral person in the American Academy of Dermatology who volunteered every Friday afternoon educating residents), and Dr. Mark Hoffman (one of the brightest minds in all of dermatology). Learning from these fine minds helped Dr. Moore attain the highest level of clinical skills in dermatology.

The passion Dr. Moore has for his specialty and his patients leads him to enjoy his work so much that he often tells his staff he feels like he is on vacation every day he works. At the same time, the primary joy of his job is the patients he is honored to care for each day. He feels humbled and appreciative of the opportunity to be a dermatologist. Dr. Moore states it is the patients, their lives, and their stories that inspire him every day to be the best he can possibly be.

Dr. Roger Moore is a board-certified dermatologist and the director and founder of the dermatology practice DermacenterMD, established in 2004. He provides a broad range of services, including skin cancer identification and treatment, Mohs micrographic surgery, general dermatology, and cosmetic rejuvenation through minimally invasive techniques. His patient following includes clients who travel from Michigan, Illinois, and Ohio, as well as Indiana to see him in Elkhart, Indiana.

A leader in skin cancer care and education, Dr. Moore has been a speaker at events in a vast geographic footprint extending from his home state of Indiana to Texas and California. He routinely teaches medical providers in his region as well as medical students through his role as the dermatology clerkship director at Indiana University Medical School in South Bend. He has also hosted nurse practitioners, physician assistants, and resident physicians for rotations through his clinic. He has contributed to research in medical dermatology and in cosmetic procedures, including botulinum toxin.

Dr. Moore founded and has been course director of Dermatology Summit, which educates and trains primary care physicians and non-dermatology providers, including nurse practitioners and physician assistants. He is also the innovator, founder, and president of Dermwise Inc., an online dermatology training platform used by dermatologists to help train their nurse practitioners and physician assistants. The Dermwise training has received endorsements from a variety of dermatology providers, most notably from Mayo Clinic graduate and past Illinois Dermatologic Society and Chicago Dermatologic Society past president Dr. Alix Charles. Dermwise has been used by dermatologists from California to West Virginia.

Dr. Moore knows the importance of continuing his own education. He maintains the highest level of continuing education, including courses from international leaders in cosmetic, medical, and surgical dermatology. He is a diplomate of the American Board of Dermatology, a fellow of the renowned American Academy of Dermatology, American Society of Dermatologic Surgery, American Society for Mohs Micrographic Surgery, and is a member of American Medical Association and Indiana State Medical Association. He takes very seriously his own knowledge and the trust his patients place in him as their provider.

He also enjoys writing his monthly newsletter, and small books like this one, to inform, entertain, and uplift his patients.

Dr. Moore knows every venture in life is not complete without family, and he is proud his wife has been the practice's administrator as well as his partner in life. He credits her for being the MVP, most valuable person, in the family and the practice. They have three children, a son and two daughters, who light up their lives.